A LITTI
M

Cynthia Cousins & Karen King
Illustrated by **Susan David**

Prepared from the archives and resources
of Shady Maple Farms.

First published in 1996 by
The Appletree Press Ltd, 19–21 Alfred Street,
Belfast BT2 8DL
Tel. +44 (0) 1232 243074
Fax +44 (0) 1232 246756
Copyright © 1996 The Appletree Press Ltd
and Shady Maple Farms.
Printed in the E.U. All rights reserved.
No part of this publication may be reproduced or
transmitted in any form or by any means, electronic or
mechanical, photocopying, recording or any information
and retrieval system, without permission
in writing from the publisher.

A Little Maple Syrup Cookbook

A catalogue record for this book is available
from the British Library.

ISBN 0-86281-623-8

9 8 7 6 5 4 3 2 1

A Note on Measures
Spoon measurements are level unless otherwise indicated.

Maple Syrup – Magnifique!

Natural sap dripping from sugar maple trees is one sure sign for many eastern Canadians and North Americans that spring has arrived. For those who grew up with sugaring-off parties, the taste of maple syrup boiled down into a thick toffee served on fresh white snow will always be a wonderful memory.

Maple Syrup: In the Beginning

It was the Native Indians who first discovered the secret of tapping maple trees to gather maple sugar. An early Native American legend tells how the god Nanabozho believed the taste of maple syrup was so extraordinary that its value would be under rated by humans if it was too accessible. So, he added water to the viscous syrup to make it watery and hid it deep inside glorious trees. Since then, getting syrup from the maple tree has been no easy task.

In the beginning, Natives collected sap from maple trees by making a diagonal cut in the trunk and inserting a bark spout in the gash. The sap flowed through the spout and was caught in birch bark buckets.

The primitive evaporation process began when the sap was poured into hollowed out basswood logs to which hot rocks were added. Slowly, the sap became a syrup, then toffee and then a crude dark sugar.

Maple sugar was the cheapest and generally the only accessible sweetener in North America until the mid-1800s. The Natives taught early pioneers how to gather the sweet maple nectar and heat it until it was concentrated into a golden amber syrup.

The simple art of gathering maple syrup was passed down through generations to become part of North America and Canada's heritage. Today, the process has become more sophisticated, but maple syrup remains a 100% pure organic product derived directly from Nature.

Maple Syrup: The Secret Within the Maple Tree

Maple syrup is made from a special seasonal secretion. This sweet water sap is different from the circulatory sap of the growing tree. The special maple sap flows in spring, when the weather shifts from freezing to thawing temperatures. If the weather remains either too warm or too cold, the maple sap will slow down or come to a standstill. For this reason, weather watching is a necessity for maple sap collection. When the climate is favourable sap may flow for as long as six weeks. Poor weather conditions may result in a short run for as little as five days. Syrup season may begin as early as March or as late as mid-April, so maple farmers must be prepared to tap the tree when nature is ready.

There are several varieties of maple trees in North America, eastern Asia and China, but it is the sugar maple which is the most productive and gives the best syrup. These trees can live to be 250 years old, but they are usually 30 years old and 10 inches (25 cm) in diameter before they can be tapped. Since tapping does no permanent damage to the tree, it may well be that some trees which were tapped by early settlers are still giving sap

today. Although the life span of the sugar maple is long, the yield is not plentiful. Each tap yields only about one litre of syrup per season.

Up until twenty-five years ago, the majority of maple producers used pails to collect their sap. Today, most producers have moved to a collection method of tubes under vacuum. These systems increase the yield without affecting the tree growth and allow tapping earlier in the season.

While today's maple syrup harvesting employs modern technology and high capacity evaporators, pure maple syrup remains an all natural unrefined sweetener.

Maple Syrup's Nutritional Content

When first tapped, maple sap is about 97% water, 3% maple sugar and 0.1% minerals. The bottled pure maple syrup is 34% water, 66% maple sugar with 40 calories per tablespoon (15 ml). Minerals in pure maple syrup include calcium, potassium, magnesium, manganese, phosphorus, and iron. Trace amounts of vitamins, including riboflavin, pantothenic acid, pyridoxine, niacin, and folic acid are also present.

Breakfast and Brunch

Turn a routine breakfast into a special treat by adding pure maple syrup. Warm up maple syrup and drizzle it over pancakes, waffles, cereal, French toast or grapefruit. Try sweetening tea or coffee by adding a teaspoon of maple syrup. Or add pure maple syrup to sour cream or yoghurt for a delicious topping for strawberries, blueberries, or raspberries.

Easy Baked Cinnamon Toast

This baked French toast puffs up in the oven to resemble a soufflé. Garnish with orange slices and strawberries for a festive, but easy, brunch.

---

2 tsp/10g butter
8 slices crusty bread, at least 1 inch /2.5 cm thick
8 eggs
1 1/4 pts/750 ml milk
6 fl oz/175 ml pure maple syrup
1/2 tsp cinnamon
1/2 tsp nutmeg
icing sugar (optional)
(serves 4)

Preheat oven to 350°F (180°C). Butter a 9 x 13 inch (22 x 32 cm) baking dish. Place the bread snugly into the baking dish adding more bread if required. Lightly beat the eggs, then stir in the milk, maple syrup, cinnamon and nutmeg. Pour the mixture over the bread. Bake uncovered for about 55–60 minutes, or until golden brown and the centre is set. Sprinkle with icing sugar or drizzle with additional maple syrup. Serve immediately.

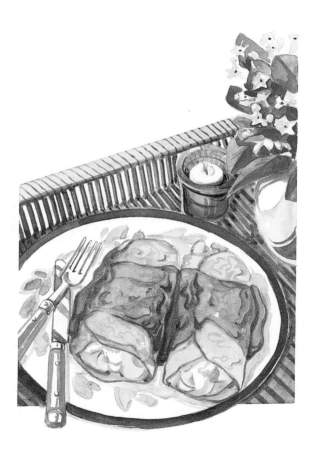

Crêpes with Ricotta and Peach Filling

The peaches and ricotta cheese team together well in these delicious crêpes.

Crêpes	Filling
5 oz/140g plain flour	5 large peaches
12 fl oz/375 ml milk	2 tbsp/25 ml butter
1 tbsp/15 ml pure maple syrup	8 fl oz/250 ml pure maple syrup
3 eggs	8 oz/240g ricotta cheese
2 tbsp/25 ml vegetable oil	2 tsp/10 ml grated lemon rind
vegetable oil for frying	
(serves 4–6)	

Crêpes: In a large bowl, whisk together the flour, milk, maple syrup, eggs and oil. Allow to stand for 10–15 minutes. Heat an 8 inch (20cm) crêpe pan or non-stick frying pan, then brush with a little oil. Pour about 4 fl oz (125 ml) of the batter into the pan, tilting to spread the batter. Cook for 1 minute until lightly brown, then turn and cook the remaining side until it is also lightly brown. Repeat until all batter is used. Stack crêpes, cover loosely, and keep warm.

Filling: Peel the peaches and slice thinly. Heat the butter and syrup in a non-stick frying pan over a medium heat. Add the peaches. Cook, uncovered, until the peaches are tender, approximately 5 minutes. Remove the peaches and keep them warm. Pour the syrup into a heatproof jug. Stir together the ricotta cheese, lemon rind and 1 fl oz (30 ml) of the syrup. Fill each crêpe with about 1 tbsp (15 g) of the cheese mixture and about 4 peach slices. Roll up and top with the remaining peach slices. Pour the remaining syrup over the crêpes and serve.

Maple Cinnamon Buns

The aroma of these cinnamon buns will evoke images of cosy, family kitchens.

4 fl oz/125 ml milk	1 tbsp/15 g dry yeast
1½ fl oz/50 ml pure maple syrup	2 eggs, beaten
4 oz/120 g butter	1¼ lb/600 g plain flour
1 tsp/5 ml salt	1 tsp/5 ml cinnamon
1 tsp/5 ml sugar	2 oz/60 g raisins and/or pecans
4 fl oz/125 ml warm water	1½ oz/50 g brown sugar

(makes 9 buns)

In a small saucepan, heat the milk, maple syrup, 2½ oz (75 g) butter and salt until lukewarm. Meanwhile, dissolve the sugar in warm water; sprinkle in the yeast and allow to stand for 10 minutes. In a large bowl, combine the milk and yeast mixtures with the eggs. Beat in 15 oz (450 g) of flour until smooth. Gradually add the remaining flour to make a soft, sticky dough. Knead on a lightly floured surface for 5 minutes or until smooth and elastic. Shape into a smooth ball and place in a large greased bowl. Cover and set aside until doubled in size, about 1½ hours. Punch down. Roll dough into an 8 x 10 inch (20 x 25 cm) rectangle. Spread with 2 tbsp (30 g) of softened butter and sprinkle with cinnamon. Cover with raisins and/or pecans. Roll up from long side and cut into 9 slices. Combine 2 tbsp (30g) of melted butter with 3 tbsp (45 g) of brown sugar in a 9 inch (25 cm) square cake pan and place the dough slices, cut side down, on top. Cover and allow to rise until doubled, approximately 45 minutes. Bake at 375°F (190°C) for 25 minutes or until golden brown. Turn immediately onto serving plate.

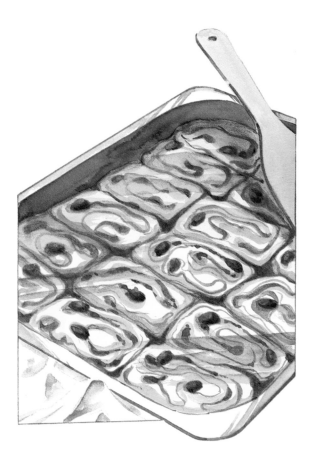

Apricot Date Loaf

A tasty loaf for brunch with the hint of maple accented by the flavour of apricots and dates.

---

5 oz/150g plain flour
3 oz/80 g whole-wheat flour
1 tsp baking powder
$^1/_2$ tsp baking soda
1 tsp salt
2 tsp cinnamon
6 fl oz/175 ml pure maple syrup
6 fl oz/175 ml buttermilk
1$^1/_2$ fl oz/50 ml vegetable oil
2 eggs, lightly beaten
1 tsp vanilla
2$^1/_2$ oz/75 g dried apricots, chopped
2$^1/_2$ oz/75 g dates, chopped
(makes 1 loaf)

In a small mixing bowl, mix the flour, baking powder, baking soda, salt and cinnamon together. In a large mixing bowl, stir together the maple syrup, buttermilk, vegetable oil, eggs and vanilla. Add the flour mixture and stir until combined. Add the apricots and dates. Pour into a well greased 9 x 5 inch (23 x 13 cm) loaf pan. Bake at 350°F (180°C) for 50 minutes or until a skewer inserted in the centre comes out clean. Cool in the loaf pan for 10 minutes, then turn onto a cooling rack.

Vegetables and Salads

Enhance the flavour of "ordinary vegetables" with pure maple syrup. The hearty flavour of cabbage, string beans and parsnips will benefit most from this unique sweet nutty taste. Combine two tablespoons each of maple syrup and butter together and use as a glaze to enhance the humblest vegetable.

In salad dressings, use maple syrup as the sweetener. Vary the dressing ingredients to create new salad sensations every day.

Maple Classic Dressing

A hint of maple flavour adds complexity to a simple dressing.

2½ fl oz/75 ml cider or balsamic vinegar
3 tbsp pure maple syrup
1 tbsp Dijon mustard
1 clove garlic, crushed
pinch of freshly ground black pepper
4 fl oz/125 ml olive oil
(makes 8 fl oz / 250 ml)

Whisk together the vinegar, maple syrup, mustard, garlic and pepper. Gradually whisk in the oil. Drizzle the dressing over salad greens and toss before serving. Refrigerate the remaining dressing.

Maple Spiced Dressing

Horseradish adds a zesty flavour to this elegant maple dressing.

2½ fl oz/75 ml red wine vinegar
3 tbsp pure maple syrup
2 tbsp horseradish
4 fl oz/125 ml vegetable oil
(makes 8 fl oz / 250 ml)

Whisk together the vinegar, maple syrup and horseradish. Gradually whisk in the oil. Drizzle the dressing over salad greens and toss before serving. Refrigerate the remaining dressing.

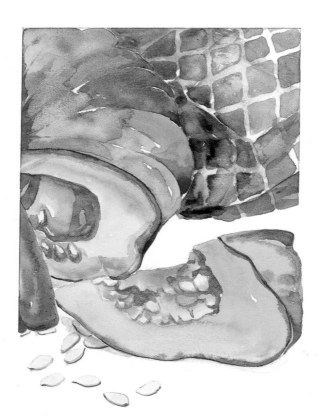

Citrus Baked Squash

For variation, you can omit the orange rind in this recipe and sprinkle each piece of squash with freshly ground nutmeg instead.

$^3/_4$ lb/875 g acorn or pepper squash
2 tsp butter
1$^1/_2$ fl oz/50 ml pure maple syrup
1 tsp orange rind, finely grated
4 fl oz/125 ml water
(serves 4)

Cut the squash in half lengthways and scoop out the seeds. Cut in half again to have four serving pieces. Place the squash pieces in a baking dish. Put $^1/_2$ tsp butter, 1 tbsp (15 ml) maple syrup and $^1/_4$ tsp orange rind into each cavity. Pour the water into the baking dish. Bake at 350°F (180°C) for 45 minutes, or until tender.

Glazed Carrots

Ginger adds heat to this simple dish, while thyme adds flavour and visual appeal.

---

1 lb/500 g carrots, cleaned and sliced thickly on diagonal
1 tbsp butter
3 tbsp pure maple syrup
$^1/_4$ tsp ground ginger
$^1/_4$ tsp thyme leaves
(serves 4)

Cook the carrots in salted boiling water for about 10 minutes until tender-crisp. Drain thoroughly. Add the butter, maple syrup, ginger and thyme to the carrots. Cook, uncovered, on a medium heat until the syrup boils. Continue cooking uncovered until the syrup is reduced and thickened and the carrots are glazed, approximately 5 minutes.

Broccoli in Maple Walnut Vinaigrette

Walnut oil adds a very distinctive flavour, but it can be replaced by corn oil if necessary.

1 large bunch broccoli
2 tbsp red wine vinegar
2 tbsp pure maple syrup
1 tsp Dijon mustard
2 tbsp walnut oil
1 1/2 oz/50 g chopped walnuts
(serves 4–5)

Wash the broccoli and cut into florets. Cook until tender-crisp in boiling, salted water. Meanwhile, whisk together the vinegar, maple syrup and mustard. Gradually whisk in the walnut oil. Place the cooked broccoli in a shallow serving dish. Pour the vinaigrette over the broccoli and sprinkle with walnuts. Serve immediately.

Four Bean Salad

Maple syrup acts as a unique sweetener in this colourful and nutritious salad.

---

¹/₄ pt/150 ml tarragon or white wine vinegar
4 fl oz/125 ml vegetable oil
2¹/₂ fl oz/75 ml pure maple syrup
1 tsp dry mustard
³/₄ tsp dried tarragon
¹/₂ tsp freshly ground pepper
1 tin (19 fl oz/540 ml) red kidney beans
1 tin (19 fl oz/540 ml) white kidney beans
1 tin (19 fl oz/540 ml) chick peas
1 tin (14 fl oz/398 ml) cut green beans
5 oz/150 g celery, sliced
1 medium sweet red pepper, chopped
2 green onions, sliced
(serves 10–12)

In a small bowl, whisk together the vinegar, oil, maple syrup, mustard, tarragon and pepper. Drain the tins of red kidney beans, white kidney beans, chick peas and green beans. Rinse the beans with cold water, then mix in a large bowl. Add the celery, red pepper and green onions. Pour the oil and vinegar mixture over the beans and mix well. Cover and refrigerate for at least 8 hours or overnight, stirring occasionally. Drain before serving.

Meat, Poultry and Legumes

Nothing beats maple syrup for glazing ham, ribs and poultry. Whether it is teamed with the piquant taste of dry mustard, orange rind or ginger, the unique flavour of maple syrup always compliments a roasted, grilled or barbecued meat dish.

As a meat marinade, maple syrup adds flavour and texture. Vary the marinade ingredients to create subtle or distinctive flavours.

Lemon Rosemary Marinated Chicken

This marinade is perfect for boneless chicken breasts. Try to use fresh rosemary as it gives the best flavour. Lime juice may be substituted for lemon juice.

2¹/₂ fl oz/75 ml lemon juice	1 clove garlic, minced
3 tbsp/45 ml vegetable oil	4 boneless chicken breasts
2 tbsp/25 ml fresh rosemary	2 fl oz/60 ml pure maple syrup
(or 1 tsp/5 ml dried)	2 tbsp/25 ml Dijon mustard

Whisk together the lemon juice, vegetable oil, rosemary and garlic. Pour the marinade over the chicken and marinate for at least 2 hours in a refrigerator. Drain the chicken, reserving marinade. Blend the maple syrup and Dijon mustard into the reserved marinade and baste the chicken frequently during grilling or barbecuing.

Peanut Grilling Sauce

Peanut sauce adds a popular Asian taste to any barbecue. Especially good with pork chops or chicken breasts.

2 oz/60 g peanut butter
2 fl oz/60 ml lemon juice or white vinegar
2 fl oz/60 ml pure maple syrup
2 cloves garlic, minced
1 tbsp/15 ml sesame oil

Whisk together all ingredients. Marinate meat or poultry in the sauce for at least 2 hours in a refrigerator. Drain and use the reserved marinade as a basting sauce during the last 10 minutes of grilling or barbecuing.

Crispy Maple Ribs

Maple syrup enhances the flavour of these succulent ribs.

3 lb/1.5 kg pork spare ribs
6 fl oz/175 ml pure maple syrup
1 tbsp/15 ml ketchup
1 tbsp/15 ml Worcestershire sauce
1 tbsp/15 ml red wine vinegar
1 clove garlic, finely minced
1/2 tsp/2 ml dry mustard
pinch of salt
(serves 4–6)

Cut ribs into serving size pieces, then place in a large saucepan and cover with water. Boil gently, covered, for about 1 hour or until tender, then drain. In a small saucepan, stir together the remaining ingredients. Bring to a boil. Pour over the ribs. Marinate in a refrigerator for about 2 hours, then remove the ribs and reserve marinade. Bake at 350°F (180°C) for 30–40 minutes, basting occasionally. Alternatively, grill or barbecue for about 15 minutes, until tender and glazed. Turn often and baste frequently with the sauce.

Zesty Chicken Wings

Perfect for casual get-togethers; drumsticks also work well in this recipe.

---

2 lb/1 kg chicken wings
4 fl oz/125 ml pure maple syrup
1 clove garlic, minced
1 small onion, finely chopped
2 tbsp/25 ml white vinegar
2½ fl oz/75 ml ketchup
1 tbsp/15 ml Dijon mustard
1 tsp/5 ml Worcestershire sauce
(serves 4)

Remove the tips from the chicken wings (reserve for making stock, if desired). Cut wings at joint into 2 pieces. In a shallow dish, combine the remaining ingredients then pour over the chicken. Marinate the chicken wings in a refrigerator for at least 4 hours, turning occasionally. Transfer the wings to a greased, shallow baking dish. Arrange in a single layer and bake at 375°F (190°C) for 35–40 minutes, basting occasionally. Alternatively, grill or barbecue the wings until thoroughly cooked.

Oriental Glazed Chicken

A perfect dish for the family or for entertaining. Serve with fluffy steamed rice and garnish with chopped green onions.

6 boneless chicken breasts	3 tbsp/45 ml white wine vinegar
3 tbsp/45 ml plain flour	2 fl oz/60 ml soy sauce
2 tbsp/25 ml vegetable oil	1 large clove garlic, minced
6 fl oz/175 ml pure maple syrup	2 tsp/10 ml ground ginger
2 fl oz/60 ml white wine	pinch of freshly ground pepper

(serves 6)

Dredge the chicken breasts with flour, then shake off any excess. Heat the oil in a large, non-stick frying pan over a medium to high heat. Brown the chicken on each side. Meanwhile, whisk together the remaining ingredients. Pour the glaze mixture over the chicken breasts. Bring to a boil. Reduce heat and simmer, covered, for 30 minutes. Turn and baste chicken.

Orange Maple Glazed Duck

This simple, yet elegant, main dish is a long-established favourite.

4–5 lb/2–2.5 kg duck	3 tbsp/45 ml pure maple syrup
pinch of salt and pepper	1 orange, reserving juice and rind

For even cooking, ensure the duck is at room temperature before roasting. Preheat oven to 450°F (230°C). Prick the duck skin with a fork so the fat will drain out. Season, inside and out, with salt and pepper and place in a shallow roasting dish. Roast, uncovered, for 30 minutes. Meanwhile, combine the maple syrup with the grated rind and orange juice. Drain the fat from the dish and reduce the oven temperature to 350°F (180°C). Continue roasting, uncovered, for 1½ hours, basting with the maple syrup mixture every 10 minutes. To test if the duck is cooked, prick the skin; juices should run clear yellow and the drumstick should move easily.

Festive Maple Glazed Ham

A holiday favourite, this maple syrup glaze is very easy to make and adds a special touch to a family meal.

4 lb/2 kg ready-to-serve ham	4 fl oz/125 ml white wine
15 whole cloves	or apple juice
2½ fl oz/75 ml pure maple syrup	4 fl oz/125 ml water
1½ tsp/7 ml dry mustard	
(serves 6–8)	

Place the ham in a shallow roasting dish, fat side up. Score the fat in a diamond pattern and insert cloves into the scored ham. Combine the maple syrup and mustard together, brush half of this mixture over the ham. Pour the wine or apple juice and water into the bottom of the roasting dish. Bake at 325°F (160°C) for 1 hour, basting occasionally with the remaining maple syrup mixture. Add more water or wine, if necessary, to keep the pan from drying.

Quebecois Baked Beans

Old fashioned, heart warming French Canadian style baked beans; a perfect "in from the cold" meal.

1 lb/500 g dried white pea beans	6 fl oz/175 ml pure maple syrup
3 pts/1.5 L cold water	4 fl oz/125 ml salsa
1 large onion, chopped	3 tbsp/45 ml molasses
4 oz/125 g salt pork or bacon	1 tsp/5 ml dry mustard
3 apples, peeled, cored, and cut in pieces	1 tsp/5 ml salt

(serves 8)

Rinse the beans and place in a large saucepan. Cover with cold water and allow to soak overnight. Then bring the beans to a boil (do not change the water). Reduce heat and simmer, covered, until tender, approximately 1 hour. Drain beans and reserve the cooking water. In a 3 pint (2.5 l) casserole or baking dish, combine the beans, onions, diced salt pork, apples, maple syrup, salsa, molasses, mustard and salt. Add just enough reserved cooking water to cover, then stir well. Cover and bake at 300°F (150°C) for 4 hours or until tender. Stir occasionally and add more water as required to keep the beans just covered. About 30 minutes before serving, remove lid to allow beans to brown.

Desserts

Why serve a dessert unless it has some magic? Let pure maple syrup create a stir of interest in the finale to your meals. Try adding a maple coulis to a simple dessert to make it special. Drizzle pure maple syrup on a plate, then swirl fresh fruit puree or yoghurt on top before adding ice cream, cake or fresh fruit.

Creamy Dessert Fondue

This delectable fondue sauce dresses up a variety of fruits, yet is a casual dessert to share among friends.

---

1 tbsp/15 ml cornflour
¹/₂ pt/300 ml single cream
4 fl oz/125 ml pure maple syrup
1 tbsp/15 ml almond or fruit-flavoured liqueur
bite-size pieces of fruit for dipping (strawberries,
apple, banana, cantaloupe)
(serves 3–4)

Whisk together the cornflour and 2 tbsp (25 ml) of cream. In a medium saucepan combine the remaining cream and maple syrup. Bring just to a boil. Add the cornflour mixture and stir until thickened. Remove from the heat and stir in the liqueur. Serve in a small dessert fondue pot with fruit arranged on a platter.

Fresh Fruit Salad with Maple Syrup

A sophisticated and elegant twist on a very simple dessert.

---

4 fl oz/125 ml pure maple syrup
3 tbsp/45 ml orange or almond flavoured liqueur or rum or cognac
1 lb/450 g fresh fruit pieces (grapefruit, orange, banana,
strawberries, cantaloupe, blueberries, kiwi fruit, etc.)
(serves 5)

Mix maple syrup and liqueur together. Gently stir maple syrup mixture into fresh fruit pieces. Allow to stand for 30 minutes to 1 hour.

Maple Nut Baked Apples

Here is a twist on a comfortable old favourite. Dried cranberries are gaining popularity and make for a colourful and delicious alternative to raisins.

4 apples
4 fl oz/125 ml pure maple syrup
1 tbsp/15 ml chopped pecans or almond slivers
1 tbsp/15 ml raisins or dried cranberries
1 tbsp/15 ml butter
1 tsp/5 ml cinnamon
water
(serves 4)

Remove most of the core of each apple, but leave a $\frac{1}{2}$ inch (1 cm) "plug" at the bottom. Set in a baking dish. Blend together the maple syrup, nuts, raisins or cranberries, butter and cinnamon. Divide mixture equally and spoon into apple cavities. Pour water around the apples to a depth of $\frac{1}{4}$ inch (6 mm). Bake at 375°F (190°C) for 45 minutes, or until apples are soft. Spoon apples and sauce into individual serving dishes. Serve with ice-cream, drizzled with maple syrup.

Maple Poached Pears in White Wine

Team this classic dessert with biscotti or other crisp biscuits.

4 firm ripe pears	1/2 pt/300 ml white wine
4 whole cloves	water
1 cinnamon stick	2 tbsp/25 ml sliced almonds
4 fl oz/125 ml pure maple syrup	

(serves 4)

Peel the pears and remove the cores but leave the stem in place. Stud a clove into each pear. Place the pears on their sides in an ovenproof dish. Place the cinnamon stick beside the pears. Blend the maple syrup and wine together and pour over the pears. Add water, if required, to ensure that the liquid is half covering the pears. Cover with foil and poach for about 1 hour at 375°F (190°C), basting occasionally. Remove cloves and cinnamon stick and spoon pears and sauce into individual serving dishes. Sprinkle with toasted, sliced almonds.

Maple Apple Blueberry Crisp

Maple syrup is the sweetener in both the filling and the crust of this delicious "comfort food" dessert.

1 lb/450 g sliced apples
1 tbsp/15 ml cornflour
1 tsp/5 ml cinnamon

> 1/2 pt/300 ml pure maple syrup
> 1/2 pt/300 ml blueberries, fresh or frozen
> 6 oz/175 g rolled oats
> 2 oz/75 g plain flour
> 4 oz/125g butter, softened
> (serves 6)

Place the sliced apples in an 8 inch (20 cm) square pan. Whisk the cornflour and cinnamon into half the maple syrup. Pour the maple syrup mixture over the apples. Add the blueberries, stirring gently to mix together. In a small bowl, stir together the rolled oats and flour. Blend in the butter. Stir in the remaining maple syrup, then spread the rolled oat mixture evenly over the apples. Bake at 375°F (190°C) for 45 minutes or until crumb topping is browned.

French Canadian Maple Syrup Pie

This traditional recipe is so rich that only small serving pieces are needed. The recipe can be easily doubled.

1 oz/30 g plain flour	2 egg yolks, beaten lightly
4 fl oz/125 ml cold water	2 tbsp/25 ml butter
1/2 pt/300 ml pure maple syrup	1 baked 8 inch (20 cm) pie shell

Stir together the flour and water until smooth. In a heavy saucepan pour in the maple syrup. Stir the flour mixture into syrup then add the beaten egg yolks. Cook over a low heat, stirring constantly, for about 5 minutes until thickened. Add the butter and stir until melted. Pour the mixture into the pie shell. Cool to room temperature before serving with whipped or ice cream.

Maple Pecan Pie with Chocolate Chunks

Melted chocolate chunks are a wonderful surprise in this delicious maple pecan pie.

3 squares (3 oz/85 g) bittersweet chocolate	3 eggs
3 oz/100 g chopped pecans	6 fl oz/175 ml pure maple syrup
1 9 inch (23 cm) unbaked, deep pie shell	1 tsp/5 ml vanilla
	2 tbsp/25 ml butter, melted

Cut the chocolate into chunks. Scatter the chocolate pieces and pecans over the unbaked pie shell. In a medium mixing bowl, beat the eggs with a whisk. Mix in the maple syrup, vanilla and melted butter and stir thoroughly. Pour the filling into the pie shell. Bake at 350°F (180°C) for 40 minutes or until centre is brown but not quite set (centre sets upon cooling). Cool on a rack.

Maple Mousse with Candied Pecans

The candied pecans in this melt in the mouth mousse add a surprise crunchy texture – sure to please.

---

2 1/2 oz/75 g pecan halves	3 eggs, separated
1/2 pt/300 ml pure maple syrup	1/2 pt/300 ml double or
1 sachet unflavoured gelatin	whipping cream
3 tbsp/45 ml cold water	6 pecan halves (optional garnish)
(serves 6)	

Toast the pecans on a baking sheet at 350°F (180°C) for 5 minutes. Heat one-third of the maple syrup in a heavy medium saucepan until boiling. Boil rapidly for 4–5 minutes, stirring occasionally. Remove from the heat and add the pecans, stirring until they are evenly coated. Remove the pecans from the saucepan and allow to cool. Cut the candied pecans into small pieces and set aside. In a small bowl, sprinkle the gelatin into the cold water then set aside. In a double boiler, mix together the remaining maple syrup and the egg yolks. Stir constantly for about 9 minutes, until slightly thickened. Add the gelatin mixture and stir until dissolved, then remove from heat. Allow to cool in a large bowl until the mixture is the same consistency as unbeaten egg whites. Beat the egg whites until stiff. Beat cream until stiff. First, fold egg whites into the maple syrup mixture, then fold in the whipping cream. Add the candied pecans and stir until combined. Divide mousse between six serving dishes, then cover and chill for 3 hours.

Maple Walnut Torte

This is a favourite in most North American homes – a very rich and decadent dessert.

Base:	3 tbsp/45 ml pure maple syrup
3 oz/90 g butter	1 tbsp/15 ml corn syrup
2 oz/60 g sugar	2 tbsp/25 ml double cream
1 egg yolk	7 oz/200 g walnuts, coarsely
5 oz/140 g plain flour	chopped and toasted
Filling:	**Topping:**
4½ oz/125 g brown sugar	6 oz/170 g semi-sweet chocolate
2 oz/60g butter	4 fl oz/125 ml double cream
(serves 8–10)	

Base: Preheat oven to 350°F (180°C). Cream together the butter and sugar until light and fluffy. Add the egg yolk and beat well. Stir in the flour until the mixture is blended and crumbly. Press firmly into a 10 inch (25 cm) springform cake tin. Ensure the mixture comes at least ½ inch (1 cm) up the sides of the cake tin. Bake for 12 minutes until lightly golden.

Filling: Combine the brown sugar, butter, maple syrup, corn syrup and cream in a heavy saucepan. Stir constantly and bring to a boil. Boil for 1 minute, then gently spread nuts over the base. Pour the filling evenly over the walnuts. Bake for 10 minutes or until bubbly. Allow to cool.

Topping: Melt the chocolate and cream together over a low heat, stirring until smooth. Spread chocolate over torte.

Cheesecake Blossom Tarts with Raspberries

For a stunning dessert, place raspberry *coulis* (*purée*) on the bottom of a dessert plate. Place the filo tart on top of *coulis* and garnish with additional raspberries.

Crust:	1 sachet of gelatin
6 sheets filo pastry, thawed	2 fl oz/60 ml cold water
2 oz/60 g butter, melted	4 fl oz/125 ml whipping cream
Filling:	12 oz/300 g raspberries,
8 oz/250 g cream cheese	fresh or frozen
6 fl oz/175 ml pure maple syrup	
(makes 12 tarts)	

Grease 12 muffin tin cups. Lay 3 filo sheets on a large cutting board and brush with some melted butter. Cut each sheet into 6 even rectangles. Fit a double layer of filo rectangles into 6 muffin cups. Then place a single rectangle into each muffin cup. Arrange the corners so they stick out in different directions and the cup is 3 filo layers thick. Repeat with remaining 6 muffin cups. Bake at 350°F (180°C) 10 minutes or until golden. Cool for 10 minutes in the muffin tins, then remove and cool completely.

Filling: Beat the softened cream cheese with an electric mixer until smooth. Blend in the maple syrup. In a small pan, pour gelatin into cold water. Allow to stand for 5 minutes. Heat gelatin over a low heat, stirring until dissolved. Add the hot gelatin to cream cheese mixture and then fold in the whipped cream. Chill the mixture for about 15 minutes. When chilled, stir, then pour about 2 oz/50 g filling into each filo "blossom". Stand for 2 hours to set. Just before serving, divide raspberries between tarts.

Index